Feelings

I'M BUSY

a feelings story

WITHDRAWN

D1357610

Clare Hibbert

Illustrated by Simona Dimitri

TULIP

TULIP
BOOKS®

www.tulipbooks.co.uk

This edition published by:
© Tulip Books 2014

First published in this edition by Evans Brothers Ltd, London in 2010.

Concept: Clare Hibbert
Editor: Clare Hibbert
Designer: Sandra Perry
Picture researcher: Sophie Schrey
Illustrator: Simona Dimitri (Milan Illustration Agency)
Sign language artist: Rob Perry

British Library Cataloguing in Publication Data (CIP) is available for this title.

ISBN 978-1-78388-042-3

Printed in Spain by Edelvives

**The signing instructions in this book follow British Sign Language.
The visual instructions show a mirror image to make it easier for
you to practise your own signing in front of a mirror.**

CONTENTS

Friendly

ahh!

Party

4

friendly   scared   busy   lonely

Scared

I imagined a real pirate coming to my party. I felt **scared**.

shiver

6

friendly   scared   busy   lonely

ahoy!

silly

excited

sorry

cheeky

special

Busy

Mmmm!

friendly

scared

busy

lonely

Lonely

My best friend Lily was too ill to come. She felt **lonely**.

Silly

tee hee!

friendly　　scared　　busy　　lonely

woo hoo!

silly

excited

sorry

cheeky

special

Sorry

bang!

 friendly

 scared

 busy

 lonely

Tyler burst Anya's balloon. But he was very **sorry**.

silly excited sorry cheeky special

17

Cheeky

chuckle

friendly

scared

busy

lonely

18

19

Special

mwa! mwa! mwa!

friendly

scared

busy

lonely

Notes for adults

The **Feelings** series has been designed to support and extend the learning of young children. The books link in to the Early Years curriculum and beyond. Find out more about Early Years and reading with children from the National Literacy Trust (www. literacytrust.org.uk).

The **Feelings** series helps to develop children's knowledge, understanding and skills in key social and emotional aspects of learning (SEAL), in particular empathy, self-awareness and social skills. It aims to help children understand, articulate and manage their feelings. Visit http://nationalstrategies.standards.dcsf.gov.uk/node/87009 to find out more about SEAL.

Titles in the series:

I'm Happy and other fun feelings looks at positive emotions
I'm Sad and other tricky feelings looks at uncomfortable emotions
I'm Tired and other body feelings looks at physical feelings
I'm Busy a feelings story explores other familiar feelings

The **Feelings** books offer the following special features:

1) **matching game**
   a border of faces gives readers the chance to hunt out the face that matches the emotion covered on the spread;
2) **signing instructions**
   each spread includes clear visual instructions for signing the emotion (these follow British Sign Language standard – visit britishsignlanguage.com for more information about this organisation);
3) **fantasy scenes**
   since children often explore emotion through stories, dreams and their imaginations, two emotions (in this book, 'scared' and 'silly') are presented in a fantasy setting, giving the opportunity to examine intense feelings in the safety of an unreal context.

Making the most of reading time
When reading with younger children, take time to explore the pictures together. Ask children to find, identify, count or describe different objects. Point out colours and textures. Pause in your reading so that children can ask questions, repeat your words or even predict the next word. This sort of participation develops early reading skills.

Follow the words with your finger as you read. The main text is in Infant Sassoon, a clear, friendly font designed for children learning to read and write. The thought and speech bubbles and sound effects add fun and give the opportunity to distinguish between levels of communication.

Extend children's learning by using this book as a springboard for discussion and follow-on activities. Here are a few ideas:

Pages 4–5: I feel friendly

Provide card and paints, pens or stickers for the children to make party invitations. Encourage them to think about possible themes before they start their designs. Ask the children what information should go on the 'writing side' of the invitation. Which friends would they like to invite?

Pages 6–7: I feel scared

Role-play being pirates. Children can raid the dressing-up box or make their own eye patches, neck scarves and toilet-roll telescopes. Sing pirate songs together. Visit http://www.singup. org/songbank/songs/view/song/66/pirates! to find the words and tune for "The pirate ship is coming".

Pages 8–9: I feel busy

With supervision, even young children can help bake a batch of fairy cakes. They can decorate them with icing, sprinkles and sweets, or make little pirate flags like the ones in the picture.

Pages 10–11: I feel lonely

Talk about how the girl in the story feels. What could the boy in this story do to help his friend feel better? Can the children remember occasions when they felt lonely or left out? What helped them feel included again?

Pages 12–13: I feel silly

Encourage the children to practise prowling and pouncing like tigers. You could provide interesting surfaces for them to move across – for example, a bristly doormat, some crackly paper or some child-safe sand. How quiet can the children be?

Pages 14–15: I feel excited

Try this guessing-game version of "Pass the parcel". Wrap objects with distinctive shapes (for example, a toy dinosaur, ship and plane; a kitchen sieve, pan and wooden spoon) in layers of old paper. Play "Pass the Parcel" the usual way, pausing to unwrap a layer whenever the music stops. Who can guess what's inside before the last layer of paper comes off?

Pages 16–17: I feel sorry

Make templates from stiff card for different-sized round and long balloons. Provide sugar paper, pencils and safety scissors so the children can draw around the templates and cut out balloon shapes in different colours. This is a great activity for improving hand-eye coordination. Why not stick all the balloons on the wall to make an eye-catching mural?

Pages 18–19: I feel cheeky

There are lots of great games that children can play with juggling or ball-pool balls. Divide children into teams and give each team a bucket and lots of small balls. Which team can throw most balls into their bucket? Count the balls together.

Pages 20–21: I feel special

Everyone has a birthday – their own special day. Make a big birthday calendar. Divide a big sheet of paper into 12 sections, one for each month. Make the background of each section relate to the season (for example, add ice crystals for January, puddles for February, spring flowers for March). Children can add themselves to the right months, sticking on their name and birth date, perhaps with a photo or drawing, too.

Sign language

busy **8**

scared **6**

cheeky **18**

silly **12**

excited **14**

sorry **16**

friendly **4**

special **20**

lonely **10**

Index

Credits

The publisher would like to thank the following for permission to reproduce their images:
iStockphoto: cover and 8–9 (TerryJ), 4 envelope (leezsnow), 6–7 (Paul Cowan), 6 (GlobalP), 7 (Kangah), 8 (dcdp), 10–11 (IrvStock), 12–13 (Macsnap), 12 (ivar), 14–15 (Devonyu), 16–17 (LeggNet), 16 (JaneB), 18–19 (Gloria-Leigh), 18 (Brian A Jackson), 20 (onurdongel); **Shutterstock Images:** 4–5 (Mastering_Microstock), 4 and 14 stickers (BooHoo), 10 (Anke van Wyk), 11 (Paul Matthew Photography), 20–21 (Mark Bonham).